LUDWIG VAN BEETHOVEN

QUARTET

for 2 Violins, Viola and Violoncello
A minor/a-Moll/La mineur
Op. 132

Edited by/Herausgegeben von
Wilhelm Altmann

T0081274

Ernst Eulenburg Ltd

London · Mainz · Madrid · New York · Paris · Prague · Tokyo · Toronto · Zürich

BEETHOVEN, STRING QUARTET IN A MINOR, OP. 132

The autograph score of op. 132—since April 1909 in possession of the State Library, Berlin—is headed:—"2tes Quartett 1825 von L. v. Bvn." It is the second of the quartets which Beethoven had promised to Prince Galitzin as far back as January 1823. The Finale, originally in D minor from the sketches made in the latter year (1823),seems to have been destined at first for the 9th Symphony. Further sketches date from the year 1824, but the work only found its final form in 1825. On March 19th Beethoven mentions it in a letter to the publisher Schott, of Mainz, declaring it nearly ready, but,the composer being rather ill in the middle of April and prevented from working for several weeks, it was August before the quartet was completed. The movement styled "Alla danza tedesca" was omitted in this work and included in the B flat quartet, op. 130. Distinct reference is made by Beethoven to his illness in this work, as we shall see.

On Sept. 9th,1825,the quartet was played by Schuppanzigh and his colleagues in the "Gasthaus zum wilden Mann", in the Prater at Vienna. To this private performance the publisher Schlesinger, of Berlin, summoned Beethoven from Baden, and obtained the publishing rights of the work for Germany and France at the cost of 80 ducats. The first public performance of the quartet took place an Nov. 6th in Vienna, at a concert given by the 'Cellist Linke. It was not printed till after the composer's death.

On page 60 of the manuscript (see page 22 of the present score) Beethoven wrote the following words:—

"2nd Movement. Thanksgiving to God by one recovering from illness, in the Lydian mode.

N.B. In this piece use is always made of

b ═══● and never the usual $b\,flat$ ═══●═

and bar 31 further on: Andante, regaining new strength."

In this edition, at the passages mentioned, the added Italian translation is written in the manuscript by a foreign hand under Beethoven's own German words.

The title of the original edition was as follows:—"Quatuor pour 2 Violons, Alto et Violoncelle. Composé et Dédié à Son Altesse Monseigneur le Prince Nicolas de Galitzin Lieutenant Colonel de la Garde de Sa Majesté Impériale de toutes les Russies par Louis van Beethoven." Oeuvre posthume. (*Then to the left in the corner*): Oeuvre 132. No. 12 des Quatuors. Propriété des éditeurs, Berlin chez A. Mt. Schlesinger, Libraire et éditeur de musique etc, Verlags-No. der Partitur 1447, der Stimmen 1443.

The following

VARIANTS

are to be noted:—

I. It is not a misprint if, in all editions save those of Holle-Liszt and Joachim-Moser, the viola part in bar 30(page 2 of the present score)instead of $b\,flat$

𝄡♭● (third quaver) reads simply

b 𝄡 . It is a mistake found in Beethoven's manuscript, the composer having clearly written $b\,flat$ in the violin part thinking it unnecessary to add it in the viola, as in the next bar it is also omitted in the 1st violin

II. In the original edition of the parts, as well as that of Ewer & Co., B. & H. and the older Peters edition the following notes stand and agree with the

M.S. In the 46th bar before the close of the 1st movement (Score page 10, brace-system IV, bar 219) in violin I

cresc.

But in the Röntgen edition the last quaver is altered to which is obviously to be preferred and approved by Joachim-Moser.

III. Ewer & Co., Holle-Liszt, as well as the old Peters Edition, 20 bars later (page 12 bar 246) in Violin I give *e* in the 3rd quaver, but the original edition and the revised one rightly give *g*, as do Joachim-Moser, following the 4th quaver with *A*. In the original it stood thus:

corrected *(e f)* by the composer in pencil.

IV. With the exception of the original edition, which corresponds with the autograph copy, all other editions (even Joachim-Moser) agree that in the movement 41 bars before L'istesso Tempo ¢ (Score page 20 bar 177) should be written

Viol. I.

instead

of

V. The somewhat capricious alteration of $\frac{1}{4}$ notes to eighths, as occurs on page 23, bar 48 (Violin II) and bar 57 (Violin I), and also in other editions, is vindicated in similar passages of the same nature. In the M.S. as well as the original edition $\frac{1}{4}$ notes prevail.

It must be noted that Beethoven on the entry of the Andante wrote

, but later altered it correctly to $\frac{6}{8}$.

VI. The alteration of the last bar but one of the Molto adagio (Score page 30 bar 210), as it appears in Röntgen's parts, and also in the London and Holle-Liszt editions

and also later preferred by Joachim-Moser, is hardly credible, although in very clear writing Beethoven proves that he intended this:

Wilh. Altmann

BEETHOVEN, STREICHQUARTETT A MOLL, OP. 132

Die autographe Partitur des op. 132 — seit April 1909 im Besitze der Staats-Bibliothek in Berlin — ist überschrieben: 2tes Quartett 1825 von L. v. Bvn. Es ist dies nämlich das zweite der Quartette, die Beethoven bereits im Januar 1823 dem Fürsten Galitzin zugesagt hatte. Das Finale, ursprünglich in d-moll nach Skizzen aus dem Jahre 1823, scheint wohl zur 9. Sinfonie ursprünglich bestimmt gewesen zu sein. Weitere Skizzen stammen aus dem Jahre 1824, aber erst 1825 wurde das Werk ausgearbeitet; am 19. März bezeichnet Beethoven es in einem Brief an den Verleger Schott in Mainz als der Vollendung nahe, doch da er Mitte April ziemlich schwer erkrankte und mehrere Wochen am Arbeiten verhindert war, rückte der August heran, bis es fertig wurde. Weggelassen wurde der später in anderer Tonart in das B-dur-Quartett op. 130 aufgenommene Satz „Alla danza tedesca". H. Riemann hat nachgewiesen, daß das Trio des Scherzos auf dem zweiten Teil der No. 11 der „Zwölf Deutschen" beruht, die Beethoven vor 1800 für die Wiener Redoutenbälle geschrieben hat. Das Scherzo ist wahrscheinlich erst nach Beethovens Krankheit entstanden, da das „dritte Stück" dieses Quartetts in den ersten Entwürfen ein ganz anderes Thema aufweist. Auf seine Krankheit hat Beethoven in diesem Quartett ausdrücklich Bezug genommen, wie wir noch sehen werden.

Am 9. Sept. 1825 wurde das Quartett von Schuppanzigh und Genossen im Gasthause zum wilden Mann am Prater zu Wien gespielt. Zu dieser Privataufführung hatte der Musikverleger Schlesinger aus Berlin Beethoven aus Baden abgeholt; ihm gelang es auch, sich den Verlag für Deutschland und Frankreich zu sichern, und zwar für 80 Dukaten. Die erste öffentliche Aufführung dieses Quartetts fand am 6. November in Wien in einem Konzert des Violoncellisten Linke statt. Im Druck erschien es erst bald nach dem Tode des Komponisten.

Auf Seite 60 des Manuskriptes (cf. unsre Part. pag. 22) hat Beethoven folgende Worte geschrieben:

„2ter Satz. Heiliger Dankgesang an die Gottheit eines Genesenen in der Lidischen Tonart.

NB. Dieses Stück hat immer h ⊜, nie wie gewöhnlich b ⊜ und ferner weiter: Takt 31 Andante, neue Kraft fühlend".

Die in vorliegender Ausgabe an den diesbezüglichen Stellen hinzugefügte italienische Übersetzung ist von fremder Hand auch im Manuskript unter die deutschen Worte Beethovens gesetzt.

Der Titel der Erst-Ausgabe lautet: „Quatuor pour 2 Violons, Alto & Violoncelle, Composé & Dédié à Son Altesse Monseigneur le Prince Nicolas de Galitzin Lieutenant Colonel de la Garde de Sa Majesté Impériale de toutes les Russies par Louis van Beethoven." Oeuvre posthume. *(Denn links in der Ecke):* Oeuvre 132. No. 12 des Quatuors. Propriété des éditeurs, Berlin chez A. Mt. Schlesinger, Libraire et éditeur de musique etc. Verlags-No. der Partitur 1447, der Stimmen 1443.

Es sind folgende

Varianten

zu erwähnen:

I. Kein Stichfehler ist es, wenn in allen Ausgaben, außer bei Holle-Liszt und Joachim-Moser, die Violastimme Takt 30 Seite 2 der vorliegenden Partitur: statt *b*  (drittes Viertel) einfach *h* gedruckt ist, wohl aber ein Fehler, der sich im Manuskript Beethovens befindet, der offenbar, weil er in den Violinen deutlich *b* vorgezeichnet hat, in der Bratsche dies für überflüssig gehalten hat, wie er denn auch im nächsten Takte bei der I. Violine das *b* nicht vorgesetzt hat.

II. Sowohl in der Original-Stimmen-Ausgabe als auch bei Ewer & Co., B. & H. und der älteren Ausgabe von Peters ist gleichlautend mit dem Manuskripte der sechsundvierzigste Takt vor Schluß des I. Satzes (Partitur pag. 10, Takt 219) die Violine I so:

notiert; in der Röntgenschen Stimmen-Ausgabe ist das letzte Achtel in abgeändert, welche Schreibweise offenbar vorzuziehen und auch von Joachim-Moser befürwortet worden ist.

III. geben Ewer & Co., Holle-Liszt, sowie die alte Peters-Ausgabe 27 Takte später (S. 12 Takt 246) in der Violine I das dritte Viertel mit *e* an; Original-Ausgabe und kritische Ausgabe haben richtig *g*, ebenso Joachim-Moser, müßten dann aber auch im vierten Viertel *a* haben; im Autograph stand ursprünglich

, woraus dann mit Bleistift *e f* (vom Komponisten) korrig. ist.

IV. Mit Ausnahme der Original-Ausgabe, die mit dem Autograph übereinstimmt,

notieren alle anderen Ausgaben (auch Joachim-Moser) im II. Satze 41 Takte vor L'istesso tempo ¢ (Part. S. 20 Takt 177)

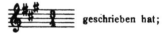

V. Die vielleicht etwas willkürliche Abänderung der $^1/_4$-Noten in $^1/_8$, wie dies in den Takten auf S. 23 Takt 48 (Violine II) und Takt 57 (Violine I) auch in anderen Ausgaben geschehen ist, rechtfertigt sich aus den Parallelstellen. Im Manuskript, sowie in der Orig.-Ausg. stehen $^1/_4$-Noten.

Erwähnenswert ist, daß Beethoven beim erstmaligen Eintritt des Andante

 geschrieben hat; später steht richtig

VI. Die Abänderung des vorletzten Taktes vom Molto adagio (Part. S. 30 Takt 210), wie sie in der Röntgenschen Stimmen-Ausgabe (gleichlautend mit der Londoner und Holle-Lisztschen Ausgabe)

und neuerdings auch von Joachim-Moser vorgenommen ist, ist kaum bedenklich, obwohl die sehr klare Handschrift Beethovens hier deutlich

zeigt.

Wilh. Altmann

Quartet

I

L. van Beethoven, Op. 132.
1770-1827

4

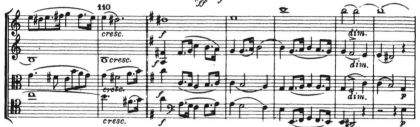

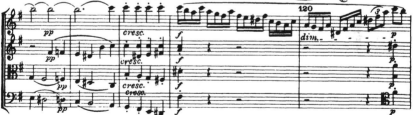

E.E. 1106

II

Allegro ma non tanto

E.E. 1106

III

Heiliger Dankgesang eines Genesenen an die Gottheit, in der lydischen Tonart.
(Canzona di ringraziamento offerta alla divinità da un guarito, in modo lidico.)

Molto adagio.

Neue Kraft fühlend.
(Sentendo nuova forza.)
Andante.

NB. Die deutschen Überschriften sind von Beethovens Hand, die italienischen von fremder Hand im Originalmanuscript geschrieben.

E. E. 1106

E. E. 1106

Molto adagio.

F.E. 1106

E.E. 1106

E.E. 1106

IV

Alla marcia, assai vivace

V

34

E.E. 1106

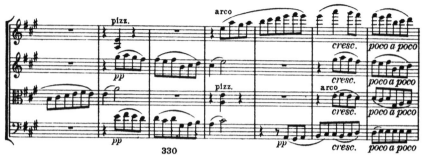